ASTRONOMY

Contents

Published in 1982 by Rand McNally & Company

First published in 1981 by Pan Books Ltd., London
Designed and produced by Grisewood & Dempsey Ltd., London

Copyright © by Piper Books Ltd. 1981
U.S. edition © Piper Books Ltd. 1982

Library of Congress Catalog Card No. 82-60154

Printed by Graficas Reunidas S.A., Madrid, Spain
All rights reserved
First printing 1982

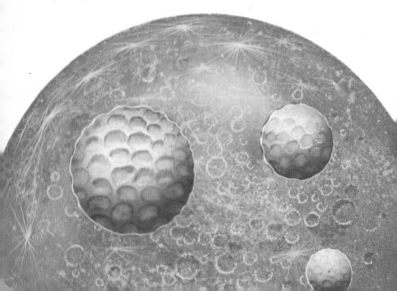

ASTRONOMY

Editor: John Paton

Series Design: David Jefferis

RAND McNALLY & COMPANY
Chicago • New York • San Francisco

Our Star, the Sun

Our sun is a star. It is like many other stars. But to everyone on earth, the sun is the most important star.

It is a ball of hot gas that gives our planet heat and light. The earth would be just a cold rock in space without the sun. There would be no air and no life.

The sun is the closest star to the earth. That's why it seems so big to us. But some stars are bigger. Others are smaller. The sun is about 93 million miles (about 150 million km)

from earth. It takes eight minutes for the sun's light to reach earth.

Light travels faster than anything else—186,000 miles (300,000 km) a second. A **light-year** is the distance that a beam of light travels in a year. We use light-years to measure how far the stars are from the earth.

Most of the sun is made of hydrogen, with 5 percent he-

(Left) The setting sun. Actually, as the earth turns around, part of it faces away from the sun.

(Below) This photo shows gas bursting out from the sun. We call this a solar eruption.

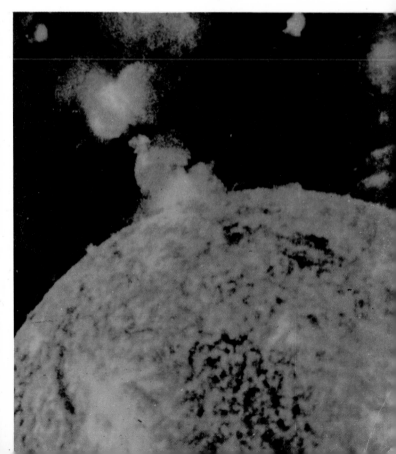

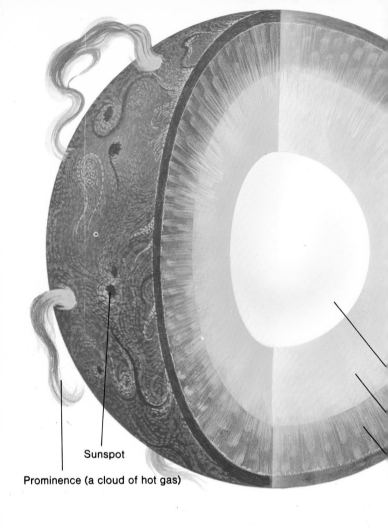

Sunspot

Prominence (a cloud of hot gas)

lium. Energy is formed at the center of the sun. It may be as hot as 27 million° F (15 million° C) at the center. The energy rises to the sun's surface. The temperature there is about 10,800° F (about 6,000° C). Energy goes out into space in the form of light and heat.

8

Photosphere (bright surface layer)

(Left) Energy is made at the center of the sun. It rises to the surface. It travels out into space in the form of heat and light.

HOW THE SUN AND PLANETS WERE FORMED

Most likely, the sun began as a cloud of cold gas and dust called a *nebula.* It began to spin slowly in space. After a while, it speeded up. It got smaller and hotter. It threw off rings of gas. Each ring of gas became a planet. The nebula eventually became the sun.

(Below) Solar flares are bursts of light on the outside of the sun. They send out different kinds of energy. Each kind travels at a different speed. *Electromagnetic radiation* travels at the same speed as light. It causes radio fade-outs. *Protons* reach the earth almost an hour later. *Electrons* do not get to earth until a day or so later. They cause *auroras.* These are bands of light in the sky at night.

Core

Rising and falling gas

Energy moving to surface

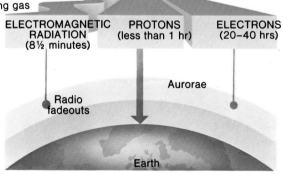

Sun

Flare

ELECTROMAGNETIC RADIATION (8½ minutes)

PROTONS (less than 1 hr)

ELECTRONS (20–40 hrs)

Radio fadeouts

Aurorae

Earth

9

Eclipses of the Sun

If a line went straight through the center of the sun from one side to the other, it would measure the sun's diameter. The sun's diameter is 400 times larger than the diameter of the moon. But the sun is 400 times farther away from us than the moon. That's why the sun and moon look the same size to us.

Sometimes the moon comes between the earth and the sun. The moon blots out the sun's light. This is an **eclipse.**

When the moon blots out *all* of the sun it is a **total eclipse.** If the moon covers

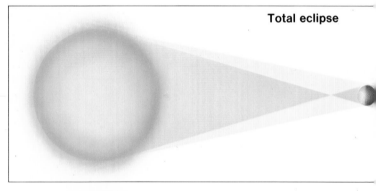

Total eclipse

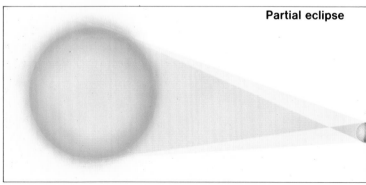

Partial eclipse

only *part* of the sun it is a **partial eclipse.**

In a total eclipse the sky gets dark. We can see a bright ring of light around the sun. It is a **halo.**

There are about two eclipses of the sun every year. They can be seen from only small areas of the earth. Astronomers travel halfway around the world to see a total eclipse.

When earth is between the sun and the moon, there is an eclipse of the moon. The moon has passed into the earth's shadow.

(Left) A total eclipse of the sun covers only a small area of the earth. A partial eclipse can be seen from a much bigger part. (Right, bottom) Partial eclipse of the moon. (Right, top) Total eclipse of the sun.

11

The Sun's Family

Nine planets revolve around our star, the sun. Earth is one of them. It is the third planet in line from the sun. The sun and everything that travels around it are called the **solar system.**

Gravity is the force that pulls things toward the center of a planet or star. It's what makes an object fall *down,* instead of go up. The sun is so big, its force of gravity is stronger than any other planet's. The planets and many other objects in the solar system spin around the sun. As they spin, the sun's gravity holds them in place.

Stars give out their own light. Planets do not have light of their own. Planets can be seen only by reflected sunlight.

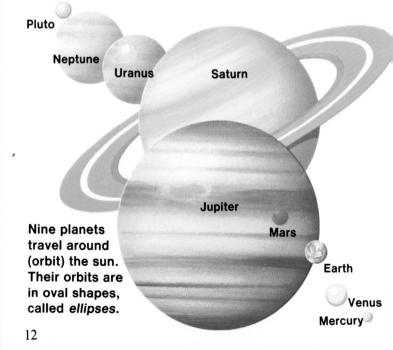

Pluto

Neptune

Uranus

Saturn

Jupiter

Mars

Earth

Venus

Mercury

Nine planets travel around (orbit) the sun. Their orbits are in oval shapes, called *ellipses.*

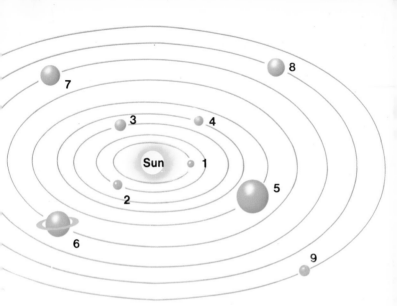

Planet	Average distance from sun (millions of miles)	Time it takes to orbit the sun	Time it takes to rotate (turn around on its axis)	Diameter (miles)
1. Mercury	35.89	88 days	59 days	3,019
2. Venus	67.08	225 days	243 days	7,526
3. Earth	92.75	365 days	23 hrs. 56 min.	7,908
4. Mars	141.4	687 days	24 hrs. 38 min.	4,216
5. Jupiter	482.5	11.9 years	9 hrs. 50 min.	88,412
6. Saturn	884.7	29.5 years	10 hrs. 14 min.	73,966
7. Uranus	1,779	84 years	10 hrs. 29 min.	30,380
8. Neptune	2,790	165 years	15 hrs. 29 min.	29,760
9. Pluto	3,658	248 years	153 hrs.	3,720?

Mercury, Little and Hot

Mercury is the planet nearest the sun. The sunshine is so bright it is hard for us to see Mercury.

In 1974 the spacecraft *Mariner 10* flew past Mercury. Astronomers found out what the surface of Mercury is like.

Not Like Home

Mercury has no air or water. The side that faces the sun reaches 780° F (416° C). This is hot enough to melt lead. The side away from the sun falls to 347° F (176° C) below zero.

Mercury looks like the moon. Both are covered with big holes, called **craters.**

Mercury speeds around the sun every 88 days. It goes about 30 miles (48 km) a second.

But Mercury rotates (turns around) slowly on its axis. (The axis is an imaginary line through the center of a planet.) It takes Earth one day (24 hours) to turn once on its axis. Mercury

A close-up of Mercury's surface. This photo was taken by *Mariner 10* in 1974.

Mercury and the
Earth. Mercury is
small but dense
(packed closely
together).
Astronomers think its
core (center) is made
of iron.

Crust

Mantle

Core

15

takes much longer—59 earth days—to rotate once.

Once in a while Mercury passes across the face of the sun. Then it looks like a small black dot on the sun. Mercury will pass across the face of the sun again in 1986.

There are wide cracks on Mercury's surface. Long ago big lumps of stone or metal hit Mercury. They were *meteorites*. They made big craters.

THE SMALLEST PLANET

Astronomers used to think Mercury was the smallest planet. But in 1980, astronomers learned that faraway Pluto was much smaller. It's only about the size of our moon.

Venus, the Hottest Planet

Venus is the second planet from the sun. But it is the hottest planet. This is because of the gases that surround it. These gases make up Venus' **atmosphere.** The chief gas around Venus is carbon dioxide. It is like the glass of a greenhouse. It heats the surface of Venus. Days can get as hot as 887° F (476° C). This is hot enough to melt lead, tin, and zinc.

Venus is about the same size as the earth. But the carbon dioxide makes the atmosphere about 100 times thicker than ours.

Bright in Our Sky

Venus looks bright in our sky. There are two reasons for this: (1) it is the planet closest to the earth; (2) it has a thick cover of white clouds that reflects sunlight.

Venus rotates once every 243 days. But it rotates backwards compared to other planets. It turns in the opposite direction. For Venus, the sun rises in the west and sets in the east!

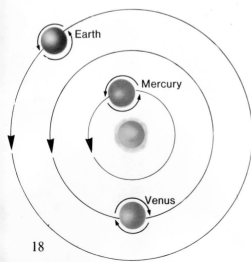

Venus does not spin on its axis in the same direction as the other planets. Venus goes the other way. It spins around once every 243 Earth days.

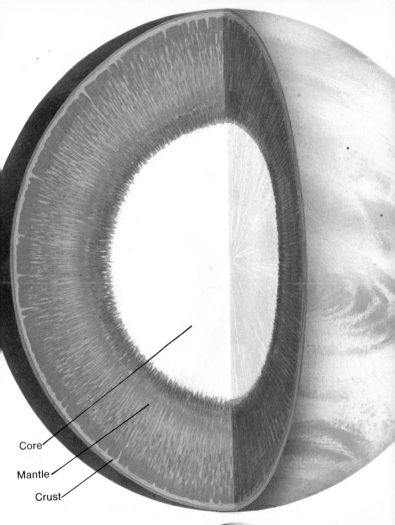

Core

Mantle

Crust

Venus is only a little
smaller than Earth. The
inside of Venus is a lot
like the inside of Earth.

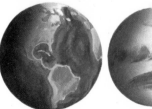

Red Mars

Mars is about half the size of Earth. Its diameter is 4,216 miles (about 6,800 km). It orbits the sun every 687 days.

In 1976 two U.S. *Viking* **space probes** landed on Mars. A probe is a spacecraft without astronauts that sends information back to Earth. The probes sent back photos. The photos showed that the surface of Mars is red. It seems to be a desert full of stones. There are many very old craters and big volcanoes.

The biggest volcano is Mount Olympus. It is the highest mountain we know about in the solar system.

Is There Life on Mars?
The *Viking* probes scooped up some of Mars's soil. No sign of anything alive was found in it. Most scientists now think there is no life on Mars. They believe there is no life on any planet in our solar system except Earth.

Core

Mantle

Crust

Mars, like Earth, seems to have a large iron core.

20

The Moons of Mars

Mars has two small satellites (moons) called Phobos and Deimos. They revolve around Mars as our moon revolves around the earth.

The U.S. *Viking* landing craft took this photo of Mars in 1976. It shows what seem to be piles of sand with rocks.

The Atmosphere of Mars

The atmosphere of Mars is carbon dioxide. It is as thin as the air 18.6 miles (30 km) above Earth. In the summer Mars's temperature falls to $-185°F$ $(-86°C)$ before dawn. In the afternoons it may reach only $-86°F$ $(-31°C)$.

The north and south poles of Mars have thin covers of frozen carbon dioxide. These white covers are called "polar caps." The polar caps get smaller when spring comes. In summer they may disappear.

The *Viking* lander must have looked like this on Mars. Is there life on Mars? The most likely place for living things would be near Mars's equator, halfway between the north and south poles. But these places were too rough for a safe touchdown. So the *Viking* had to land in the desert.

Jupiter the Giant

Jupiter is the biggest of all the planets. It weighs 2½ times as much as all the other planets put together. Its diameter is 88,412 miles (142,600 km). This is more than eleven times the diameter of the earth.

There is a thin ring of rocks around Jupiter. This ring can't be seen from earth.

Jupiter spins on its axis faster than any other planet. It spins once in 9 hours and 50 minutes. This is 2½ times as fast as the earth spins. Jupiter spins so fast that it bulges at its equator. Its poles are flat.

A Big Ball of Gas

When you look at Jupiter through a telescope, you see a lot of clouds. A sea of gases is under the clouds. The chief gas is hydrogen. Nearer to the center the gases get thicker. Then they change into liquid. There may be a small rocky core.

Have you ever heard of the Great Red Spot on Jupiter? It is a big red oval more than 18,600 miles (30,000 km) long. This spot is big enough to swallow the earth.

The Great Red Spot was first seen through telescopes in 1666. No one knew what it was until 1979. Then, two *Voyager* space probes flew close to Jupiter. The probes found that the Great Red Spot was a spinning cloud.

Astronomers think that Jupiter may be caving in.

The diameter of Jupiter is eleven times the diameter of the earth. But most of Jupiter is gas. The chief gas is hydrogen. Near the center the hydrogen is liquid. Jupiter may have a core of rock. The picture on the left shows how Jupiter would look if we were on one of its moons.

25

Jupiter has sixteen moons. Ganymede and Callisto are two of them. The diameter of each of these is bigger than the diameter of Mercury. In 1979 the *Voyager* space probe found volcanoes on Io, another moon. The volcanoes were erupting. Salt and sulfur cover the outside of Io.

(Below) Jupiter has sixteen moons. Before 1979 only thirteen moons were known. Their orbits are shown below. Two of these moons are Ganymede and Callisto.

Each of these is bigger than the planet Mercury. (Right) In 1974 *Pioneer 11* took this photo of Jupiter. A spinning cloud called the Great Red Spot is near the center.

Looking at Jupiter

Jupiter is one of the most interesting planets to watch. It is so big that we can see it with binoculars. If we look through a telescope of low power, we will see light and dark bands of cloud. Some of these change every week or month. But the Great Red Spot stays the same.

When Jupiter is nearest Earth, it is about 397 million miles (640 million km) away. Then we can see Jupiter without binoculars.

Ringed Saturn

Saturn is the sixth planet from the sun. It is the second biggest planet. Only Jupiter is bigger. And Saturn is second to Jupiter in rotation speed. Saturn spins around once every 10½ hours. It takes 29½ years to orbit the sun. At times we can see Saturn without binoculars.

The Rings
Many people say Saturn is the most beautiful planet. It has hundreds of shining rings around it. The rings are millions of small particles. Ice coats these particles, so they are very bright.

Saturn's rings are about 170,500 miles (275,000 km) from one side to the other. But each one is only about 6.2 miles (10 km) thick.

It's Light
Saturn is so light, it would float in a big sea. Almost all of Saturn is liquid hydrogen.

A view of Saturn from its largest moon, Titan.

Astronomers think the center of Saturn is rock covered by ice.

Saturn's Moons

Saturn has more than twenty-one moons, or satellites. One of these is Titan. Astronomers think it's the biggest moon in the solar system. It is bigger than Mercury. It is only a bit smaller than Mars.

Voyager 1 found that most of Titan's atmosphere is nitrogen, like the earth's.

(Right) Saturn's rings. The second set of rings is about 17,360 miles (28,000 km) wide. The dark set nearest Saturn is about 1,860 miles (3,000 km) wide.

(Below) A photo of Saturn's rings. They are made of millions of small icy particles.

Uranus, the Green One

Uranus is a cold ball of gas. Its diameter is four times the diameter of the earth.

William Herschel, an English astronomer, discovered Uranus in 1781. In 1977 it was found that Uranus, like Saturn, has rings around it. If we look at Uranus through a telescope, it looks green. Uranus has a lot of methane, a gas, that gives it this color.

Uranus takes 84 years to orbit the sun. Unlike other planets, Uranus lies on its side as it spins. First one pole and then the other points straight at the sun. This means that a big part of Uranus has daylight for about 40 years! Then night comes for 40 years.

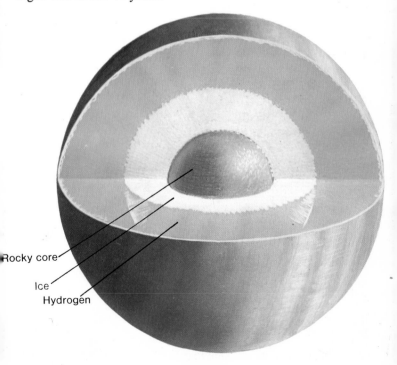

Rocky core

Ice

Hydrogen

Neptune and Pluto

Neptune was discovered in 1846. Scientists think Neptune has a big rocky core covered with ice.

Neptune is 2.8 billion miles (4,500 million km) from the sun. It takes 165 years to orbit the sun. Astronomers think that the surface of Neptune is −438° F (−221° C).

Pluto Is Far Away

Pluto was discovered in 1930. It is the smallest planet. It is smaller than our own moon. Most likely, it's only a lump of frozen gas.

Pluto takes 248 years to orbit the sun. Its orbit crosses the path of Neptune. So, for part of its orbit, Pluto is closer to the sun than Neptune is. Now, Pluto is closer to the sun than Neptune. It will be closer than Neptune until the year 2009.

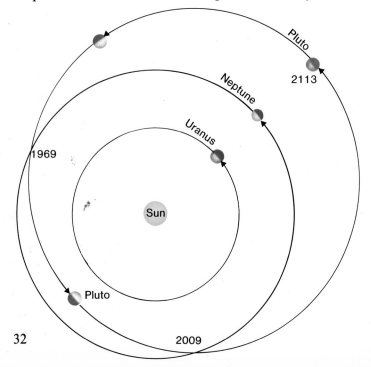

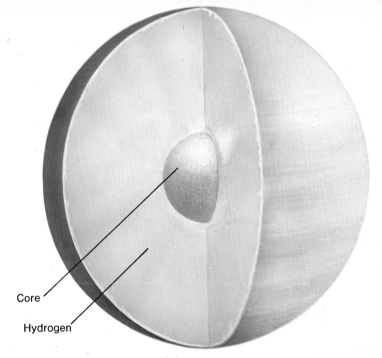

Core

Hydrogen

(Above) Little is known about what Pluto is made of. It may have an iron core like the earth's.

(Right) These photos were taken in 1930. One photo was taken three days after the other. Every star in both photos was in the same place. But the planet Pluto moved.

(Left) Between 1969 and 2009, Pluto will be closer to the sun than Neptune.

Asteroids, Comets, and Meteors

Asteroids are a group of rocks that orbit between Mars and Jupiter. Most of them travel in a big circle. This is called the **asteroid belt.** But some go far away from this belt. Asteroids were formed when the rest of the solar system began.

There seem to be about half a million asteroids larger

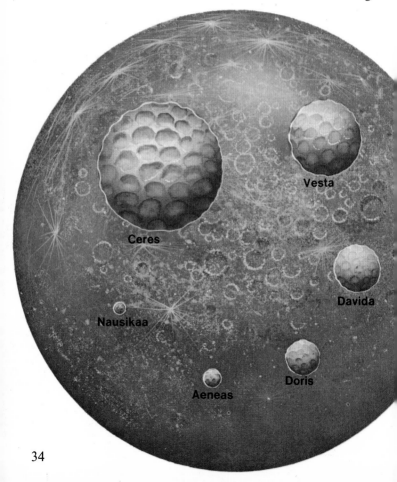

than .9 mile (1.5 km) in diameter. Ceres is the biggest asteroid. Its diameter is about 620 miles (1,000 km). Ceres orbits the sun in 4.6 years.

Astronomers think asteroids are lumps of rock with many different shapes. A few asteroids are bright enough to be seen through telescopes of low power.

Ceres was the first asteroid to be found. Guiseppe Piazzi discovered it in 1801. By 1807, Pallas, Juno, and Vesta were found.

(Left) This drawing gives us an idea of the size of some big asteroids. The moon is in back of them.

(Below) Most asteroids orbit between the orbits of Mars and Jupiter. This is the asteroid belt. But some asteroids wander far away.

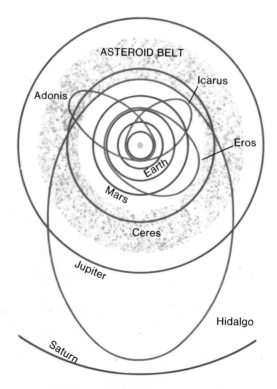

Comets

Comets orbit the sun. Their orbits are very long and strange. At regular times they pass close to the sun. But mostly they travel in the outer parts of the solar system. It is cold and dark there. The comets can't be seen because they are far away from the sun.

Comets are made of dust, ice, and frozen gas. When they come near the sun, they get warm. Their dust glows. Gas

Comet West was seen in 1976 over Kitt Peak National Observatory, Arizona.

streams away from the head of the comet. The gas forms a tail that may be millions of miles long.

Orbits of the Comets

Some comets orbit only in our solar system. One of these is Halley's comet. It never travels out as far as Pluto. Every 76 years it passes close to the sun. Then, we can see it without

using binoculars. It was seen last in 1910. It will appear again in 1986. The New Testament of the Bible tells about "The Star in the East." People once thought it was Halley's comet.

Other comets travel farther than Pluto. They are not seen often. Kohoutek's comet is one of them. In 1974 it came within 74 million miles (120 million km) of the earth. It will not come back for another 75,000 years.

Millions of Comets

There could be as many as 100 billion comets flashing around the solar system. We will not see many of them. They pass close to the sun only once in several million years.

We can see about five comets a year from earth. Most of them are not bright. So we need a telescope. But some are so bright they have been seen in daylight.

There have been only a few very bright comets in the 1900s. Halley's comet of 1910 was the brightest. There were five very bright comets in the 1800s.

(Left) Here is a picture of part of the Bayeux tapestry. It shows King Harold of England in 1066. He is on his throne. William the Conqueror is trying to take over England. Halley's comet is over the throne.

(Right) This drawing shows that orbits of some comets are short. Others are much longer. Encke's comet takes only 3.3 years to orbit the sun. This comet goes past Mars. But it does not go as far as Jupiter. Halley's comet goes almost to Pluto. It orbits the sun every 76 years. We will see it again in 1986. Kohoutek's comet will not be seen for at least 75,000 years.

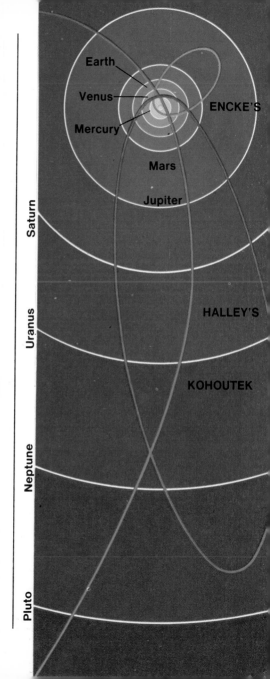

Meteors

Look at the sky for a while on any dark night. You will probably see a bright streak of light. This is a **meteor,** or shooting star. Meteors are

pieces that have broken away from comets. They can be as small as a grain of sand. They can be big enough to weigh several tons.

When meteors enter the earth's atmosphere at high

speeds, they burn up in a streak of light. This happens between 50 and 74.4 miles (80 and 120 km) above the earth.

Most of the year, meteors appear anywhere in the sky at any time. But sometimes

The largest known meteorite crater on earth is in northeastern Arizona. The Barringer or Coon Butte crater is about .74 miles (1.2 km) across and 191.4 yards (175 m) deep.

there are very many meteors at once. They dart across the sky in one direction. These meteor showers happen when the earth passes through the pieces left by broken comets.

Rocks from Outer Space

Small meteors burn up long before they get to earth. But big meteors reach the earth.

When a meteor reaches the surface of the earth, it is called a **meteorite.** Meteorites look like bright balls of fire. They travel faster than the speed of sound. This causes an explosion called a **sonic boom.**

Most meteorites don't damage anything when they land on earth. They are too small, and they travel too slowly. But sometimes windows and roofs are smashed.

Once in a long while, very big meteorites fall and make huge craters. In the desert of Arizona, there is a crater 0.74 mile (1.2 km) across. It is 191.4 yards (175 m) deep. It seems to have been made about 25,000 years ago by an iron meteorite.

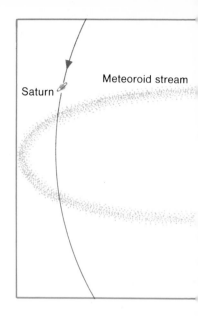

Spotting Meteorites

Very few of us will ever see a meteorite on its way to earth. When one does come, it's a very important event. Astronomers try to find pieces of the fallen meteorite. They want to find out what minerals and rocks are in them.

Meteorites seem to have helped shape the surfaces of the moon, Mars, and Mercury. These are covered with many craters.

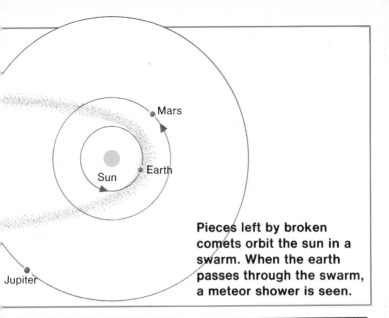

Pieces left by broken comets orbit the sun in a swarm. When the earth passes through the swarm, a meteor shower is seen.

Iron or Stone?

There are two kinds of meteorites: (1) those made mainly of stone (they are **aerolites**); (2) those made mainly of metal (they are **siderites**).

(Left) This photo shows the track of a meteor in the night sky. The arcs show trails of stars. Actually, the earth is rotating, not the stars.

43

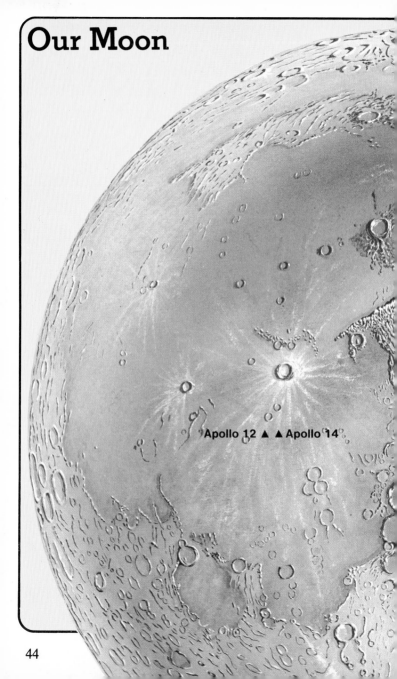

Our Moon

Apollo 12 ▲ ▲ Apollo 14

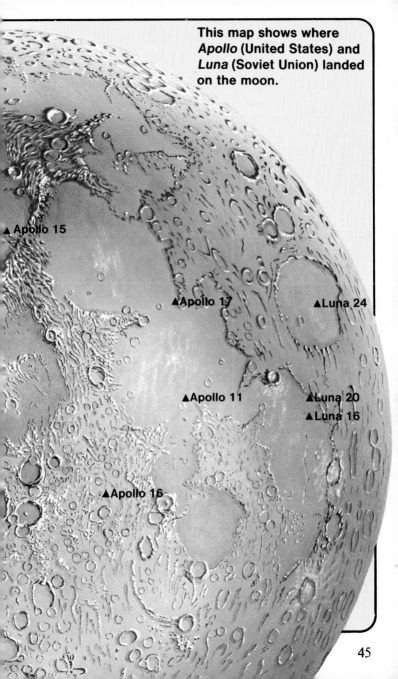

This map shows where *Apollo* (United States) and *Luna* (Soviet Union) landed on the moon.

▲Apollo 15

▲Apollo 17

▲Luna 24

▲Apollo 11

▲Luna 20

▲Luna 16

▲Apollo 16

The moon is the earth's closest neighbor in space. It is the earth's only satellite. It takes one month for the moon to orbit the earth once. The moon's orbit is in the shape of an oval (**ellipse**).

Facts About the Moon

The moon does not give off any light of its own. When it seems to shine, it is reflecting (throwing back) light from the sun.

Different parts of the moon are lit up as it travels around the sun. On some nights the moon looks like a full circle. On other nights it looks like a thin curve. The different shapes of the moon are its **phases.**

As the moon orbits the earth, the same side always faces us. That is because the

New Moon

Crescent phase

Gibbous phase

SUN'S RAYS

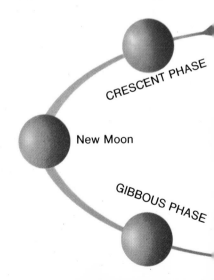

CRESCENT PHASE

New Moon

GIBBOUS PHASE

The moon is eclipsed when the earth's shadow falls on it. If the moon passes through the thin cone of deep shadow, there is a total eclipse.

The moon's phases as it orbits the earth

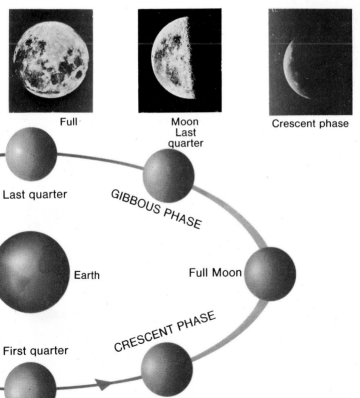

Full

Moon
Last
quarter

Crescent phase

Last quarter

GIBBOUS PHASE

Earth

Full Moon

First quarter

CRESCENT PHASE

moon takes just as long to orbit the earth as it does to spin on its axis. This is a little more than 27.3 days.

The surface of the moon has many meteorite craters. But we did not know anything about the far side of the moon until 1959. Then a Russian spacecraft took the first pictures of that side. They showed that the far side is even rougher than the near side.

Gravity on the surface of the moon is low. The moon's gravity is not strong enough to hold an atmosphere around it. So the moon has no weather and no sound. Temperatures go as high as 212° F (100° C). They go as low as −302° F (−150° C). The moon has no water or life. It is just a dead ball of rock.

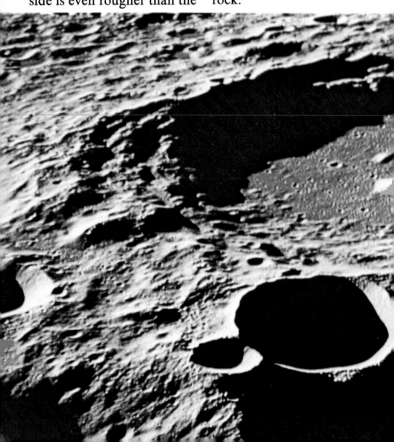

Australia is 2,340 miles (3,-744 km) from east to west. The diameter of the moon is about the same.

A close-up of the far side of the moon. The large crater is 48 miles (76.8 km) across. There are mountain peaks in the center of the crater.

Finding Out About the Moon

The earth and moon must have been made about the same time—4.6 billion years ago. Then, the solar system was full of flying pieces of rock. These pieces dug craters on the moon and earth.

The moon cooled down fast and formed a thick outer shell of rock. Most of the old craters are still there.

The earth is much bigger than the moon. So the earth stayed warm. The craters have been worn away by wind, rain, and movements of the earth's crust.

(Below) Astronaut Harrison Schmitt takes samples of the moon's soil during the final *Apollo* mission.

(Right) Schmitt works beside a huge rock on the moon. Do you see the lunar (moon) rover?

The *Apollo* Landings

Between 1969 and 1972, twelve *Apollo* astronauts landed on the moon. They spent a total of 166 hours on the moon.

The astronauts set up stations that send information to the earth. They also brought rocks and soil back to the earth. Scientists are still studying them. They may help us learn how the moon and earth were made.

Life and Death of a Star

Astronomers think that a star begins its life as a huge, thin cloud of hydrogen and other particles. The cloud is cold, dark, and possibly as big as our solar system.

The cloud begins to cave in. Pieces of dust and gas collide, giving out heat. The cloud caves in some more. Gravity at the center pulls in the rest of the cloud. The pieces of dust and gas come closer together. The center gets so hot that it begins to shine. Hydrogen begins to

Thousands of stars. A man-made satellite, passing by, made the streak across the photo.

change into helium. This makes a lot of energy. A star is born.

It may take 20 million years for all this to happen. Then the star may glow for thousands of millions of years. That's what our sun is doing. Then the star begins to use up hydrogen faster. The star gets bigger and cooler. It becomes a **red giant.**

In thousands of millions of years, our sun will become a red giant. On the earth, polar ice will melt. Lands will flood. Oceans will dry up. There will be no more life on the earth. The sun may grow large enough to swallow Mercury, Venus, and the earth.

The Death of a Star
Some red giant stars get very hot and bright and then they explode. A star that explodes is called a **supernova.**

Most stars do not explode. They get smaller until they are very dense (thick). They become **white dwarfs.**

When our sun becomes a white dwarf, it may be about the size of the earth. But it will be very dense. A spoonful of the sun's material will weigh about 10 tons! Stars may stay as white dwarfs for millions of years before they die.

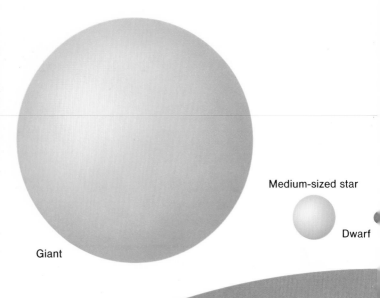

Medium-sized star

Dwarf

Giant

Supergiant

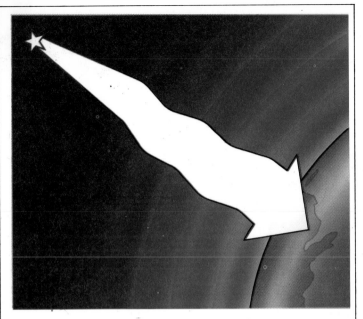

Why Do Stars Twinkle?

Stars don't really twinkle, but they look like they do. That's because we see the starlight through moving layers of the earth's atmosphere.

Stars are many different sizes. Most are like our sun. But some have become giants or supergiants. When they die, they get smaller. They become white dwarfs.

What's in Starlight

To learn more about stars, astronomers use a **spectroscope.** A spectroscope separates starlight into bands of color, like a rainbow. This rainbow is called a **spectrum.**

The gases inside of a star like our sun are under great pressure. They give off white light. Through a spectroscope,

Unbroken Spectrum

Glowing gases inside stars are squeezed together. They are under great pressure. They give off white light. The light has an unbroken spectrum (above). Glowing gas at low pressure gives a bright-line spectrum (below)

Emission (sending out) Spectrum

White light passes from inside of a star through the cooler gases of the atmosphere. Here the pressure is lower. Some light waves are absorbed. Dark lines appear in the spectrum (below).

Absorption (taking in) Spectrum

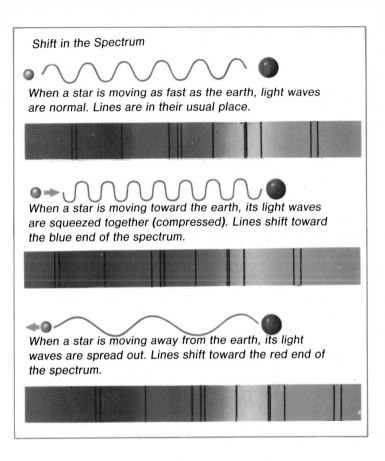

Shift in the Spectrum

When a star is moving as fast as the earth, light waves are normal. Lines are in their usual place.

When a star is moving toward the earth, its light waves are squeezed together (compressed). Lines shift toward the blue end of the spectrum.

When a star is moving away from the earth, its light waves are spread out. Lines shift toward the red end of the spectrum.

this light makes a rainbow, or spectrum. But this spectrum has dark lines. Where do these dark lines come from?

When white light passes through the cooler, lower-pressure atmosphere of a star, some light waves are absorbed (taken in). Wherever light waves are absorbed, dark lines appear in the spectrum. The positions of the dark lines tell scientists what chemicals are in the star's atmosphere.

All Kinds of Stars

Long ago the Greeks measured the brightness of stars. They put the stars that we can see without a telescope into six groups. These groups are called **magnitudes**. The magnitudes were 1st, 2nd, 3rd, 4th, 5th, and 6th.

Today we use these same groups to classify stars. The brightest stars are of the 1st magnitude. Stars that are the hardest to see are of the 6th magnitude. The brighter the star, the lower its magnitude.

The very brightest stars have magnitudes less than zero. Sirius is the brightest star in the sky. Its magnitude is −1.45. Stars that can only be seen with a telescope have magnitudes above 6. The biggest telescope can pick up stars with a magnitude of less than 20.

But how bright a star *looks* has nothing to do with how bright it really *is*. A star may be small. But if it is close to us, it seems big and bright. A star that is very big, but far away, may look dim and small.

Stars that Change

Some stars change in brightness. Often these are stars that are getting bigger. They will become red giants. The amount of light they send out changes each night or each week.

Double Stars

Many stars are in pairs called **binary systems**. The

(Right) A binary or double star system is made of two stars that revolve around each other. Algol is a double star that eclipses. One of Algol's stars is brighter than the other. Every 68.8 hours the dark star eclipses the bright one. The graph shows how much the starlight is reduced during an eclipse.

(Below, right) *Nebulae* are clouds of glowing gas and dust left after a star explodes. This picture shows the Ring Nebula in Lyra.

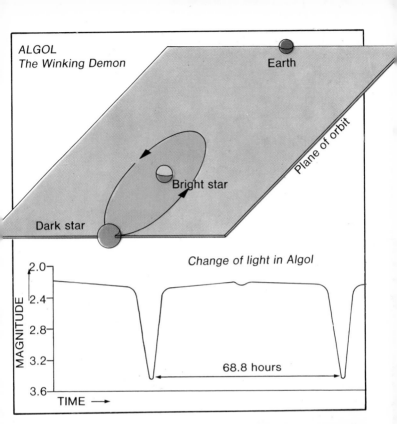

ALGOL
The Winking Demon

Earth

Plane of orbit

Bright star

Dark star

Change of light in Algol

68.8 hours

MAGNITUDE

2.0
2.4
2.8
3.2
3.6

TIME →

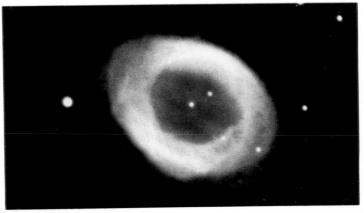

two stars revolve around each other. Astronomers have found that nearly half of all stars are binaries. The stars in binaries can be close to each other. Some stars are *very* close together.

Gravity causes hot gases to stream from one star to the other. Other stars are as far apart as the width of the solar system. If we look at these far-apart stars through a telescope, they do not seem to belong together.

Eclipse of Double Stars

In some binary systems, one

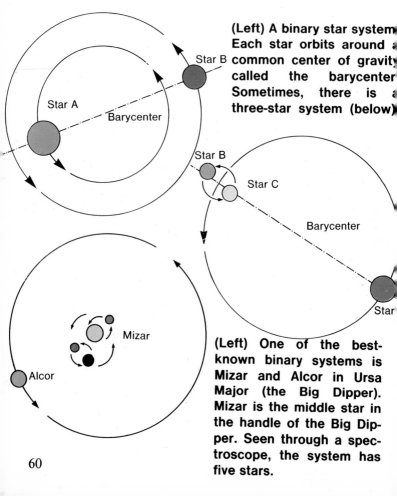

(Left) A binary star system. Each star orbits around a common center of gravity called the barycenter. Sometimes, there is a three-star system (below).

(Left) One of the best-known binary systems is Mizar and Alcor in Ursa Major (the Big Dipper). Mizar is the middle star in the handle of the Big Dipper. Seen through a spectroscope, the system has five stars.

star periodically blocks (eclipses) the light of the other.

A star, or any object, is made of **matter.** The amount of matter an object has is called **mass.** Astronomers measure the mass of stars by studying double stars. From

(Above) This cluster of stars, called Pleiades, is one of the brightest groups of stars.

their movements, astronomers can figure out the mass of each.

61

The Milky Way

Our sun is just one among 100 billion stars in our **galaxy.** A galaxy is made of millions and millions of stars. On a clear night we can see a few thousand stars without a telescope. There are so many stars in parts of our galaxy that they look like a band of light. We call this the Milky Way. When we look up at the Milky Way we are looking through the thickest part of our galaxy.

If we were in outer space, we would see that our galaxy is shaped like a flat spiral or coil. The stars branch out from the center, making wide curves. (See picture, this page.)

Astronomers think there could be a huge **black hole** in the center. A black hole is thought to be a collapsed star with very strong gravity. Nothing can escape the gravity of a black hole, not even light. Everything near the center of our galaxy may be vanishing into the black hole.

Huge Clouds of Gas

Huge clouds of gas and dust can be found in parts of the galaxy. Most of these clouds are in the galaxy's spiral

(Below) If we were above our Milky Way, it would look like a coil. From the side, it would look like a pancake. The sun is in one of the spiral "arms." The arrows show where the sun is in the Milky Way.

"arms." The clouds are called **nebulae.** New stars may be made from nebulae.

A nebula can be hundreds of light years from one side to the other. But the hydrogen and other things in it are very light. So a nebula as big as the earth would weigh only a few pounds!

(Below) The Orion Nebula looks like it's on fire. Orion is 1,500 light years away. It is about 16 light years across.

(Right) There are different types of galaxies: elliptical (oval) shaped (1); spiral (coiled) (2, 4); barred spiral (3, 5). Number 6 does not have any regular shape.

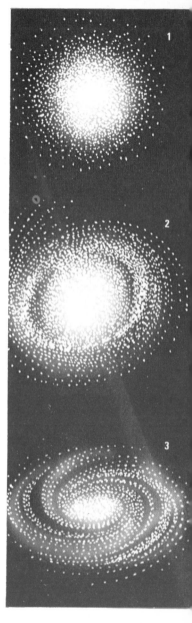

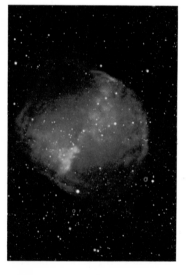

(Above) This nebula has the shape of a dumbbell. That's why it's named Dumbbell. It is about 700 light years away.

Beyond the Milky Way

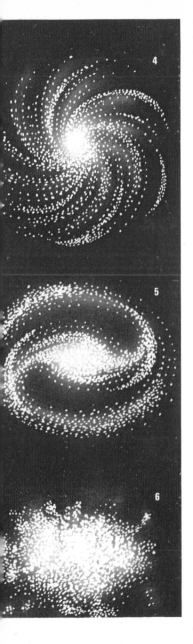

William Herschel was a famous English astronomer. In the 1700s he said that some nebulae were not what they seemed to be. He thought they might be other galaxies.

In 1917 astronomers found that Herschel was right. They turned the new giant telescope at Mount Wilson, California, on the Andromeda "nebula." They could see it was made of stars.

Astronomers found out that the Andromeda Nebula was a huge galaxy of stars. It is hundreds of thousands of light years from the earth.

A Universe of Galaxies

Astronomers have found that most galaxies are in groups. The very big Andromeda galaxy is just one in about twenty that make up our own group. Beyond ours, there are so many other groups of galaxies that we can't count them.

The universe extends much farther than we can see. With telescopes we can see no farther than about 8 billion light years away.

How Far?

Some galaxies are so far away, it is hard to figure out the distance. The best way to figure this out is by studying the red shift in the spectrum of their light. Page 56 tells about this.

The red shift shows that all the faraway galaxies are shooting away from us. They are also shooting away from each other. The farther a galaxy is from us, the faster it is traveling. This seems to tell us that the universe is getting bigger and bigger. Perhaps the universe is flying apart because of an explosion that happened long ago. Scientists call this the **big bang theory.**

Kinds of Galaxies

No two galaxies are the same. Edwin Hubble spent many years studying them. In the 1920s, he put them into these classes: (1) ellipti-cal (oval shaped); (2) spiral (coiled); (3) barred spiral. (See drawings on pages 64 and 65.) Other galaxies don't have a regular shape. So they are called "irregular."

More than half the galaxies we know about are spirals. Our own Milky Way and the Andromeda are spiral galaxies.

One-fourth of the galaxies we know about are barred. Most other galaxies are elliptical. We can see two irregular galaxies without a telescope. These are the Large and Small Magellanic Clouds. They were named for the explorer Ferdinand Magellan. They are less than 200,000 light years away.

(Right) This is the Andromeda galaxy. It is the nearest spiral galaxy to our own Milky Way. Andromeda and the Milky Way seem to be about the same size.

Quasars and Pulsars

A **quasar** is a strange object that gives off energy in the form of light and radio waves.

To us quasars look like pinpoints of light. Quasars are so far away that their light has taken billions of years to get here. This light left the quasar early in the history of the universe.

Strange Pulsars

Stars are not always entirely destroyed in a supernova. Sometimes the tiny core is left. It is squeezed very small and becomes more dense than a white dwarf. It is called a **neutron star.** It may be only 12 miles (19.2 km) across. But a tablespoonful would weigh 1 billion tons! These neutron stars send out radio waves. The waves come at regular times, like the pulse you can feel in your wrist. That's why they are called **pulsars.**

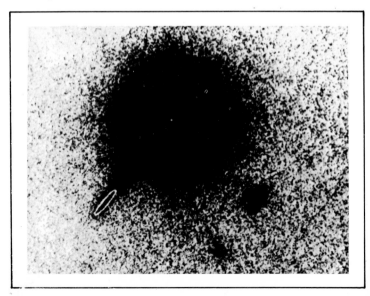

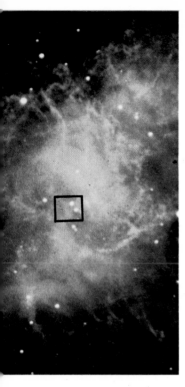

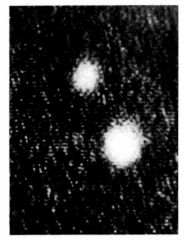

Photographs show that the Crab pulsar is "off" nearly all the time. (It doesn't send out light and radio waves.) Photo above shows the pulsar "on." Photo below shows it "off."

(Above) The Crab Nebula in Taurus is one of the most interesting objects in the heavens. It has a pulsar. The pulsar pumps out energy in the form of radio waves, light, and X rays.

(Left) This is a negative photo of a quasar that sends out strong radio waves.

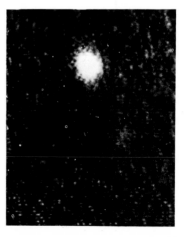

Was there a big bang billions of years ago? Most scientists think that's how the universe began.

Huge clouds of gases shot out. They cooled. Slowly, they formed galaxies.

How Did It All Begin?

How did the universe begin? We may never know for sure. But scientists have offered some interesting answers.

Georges Lemaître was a Belgian priest and an astronomer. In the 1930s he developed the "big bang" theory. He knew that all the faraway galaxies are flying away from each other. He showed that they were close together about 20 billion years ago. There may have been a "big bang." Everything at the center of the universe shot out. Then galaxies were formed.

In 1948 scientists suggested another theory. They said that faraway galaxies are moving away. But new matter is being made all the time. This keeps the universe's density (thickness) the same all the time.

Another possibility is the "oscillating universe" theory. (See below.) Oscillating means moving back and forth.

Most scientists think the big bang theory is right.

THE OSCILLATING UNIVERSE

Some scientists think the universe gets smaller, then bigger, and then smaller. They think it is getting bigger now. At some time, it will stop. It will get smaller. Then there will be another big bang. Everything will start over again. But there is no sign now that the universe will ever stop getting bigger.

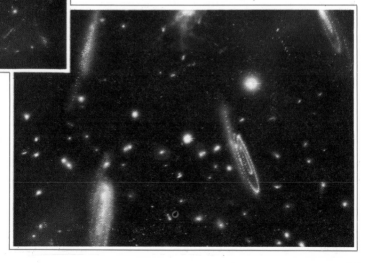

Telescopes

A telescope can collect (focus) more light than our eyes can. That's why we can see things with telescopes that we could not see with just our eyes.

There are two main kinds of telescopes—**refractors** and **reflectors.**

A telescope that refracts uses a lens to collect light. Binoculars work the same way. But it's hard to make very big lenses. That's why most big modern telescopes are the kind that reflect. They have a mirror instead of a lens.

The biggest telescope in the world is the reflector in

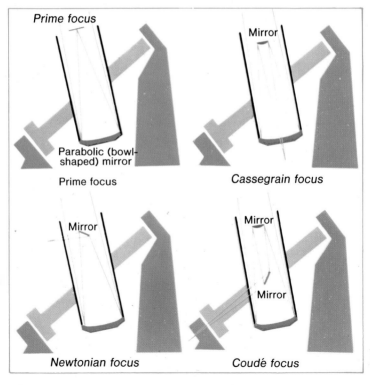

Prime focus

Parabolic (bowl-shaped) mirror

Prime focus

Mirror

Cassegrain focus

Mirror

Newtonian focus

Mirror

Mirror

Coudé focus

the Caucasus Mountains, USSR (Russia).

Radio Telescopes

Radio waves are like light waves, but we can't see them. Radio telescopes pick up radio waves from space. Most of these telescopes have big dishes. These dishes collect (focus) the radio waves. The radio sound is then made stronger (amplified).

(Above) The huge bowl of the radio telescope at Effelsberg, West Germany. It is 110 yards (99 m) across. The biggest radio dish is in Arecibo, Puerto Rico.

(Left) Four ways that reflecting telescopes bring light to focus (collect or bring to a point).

73

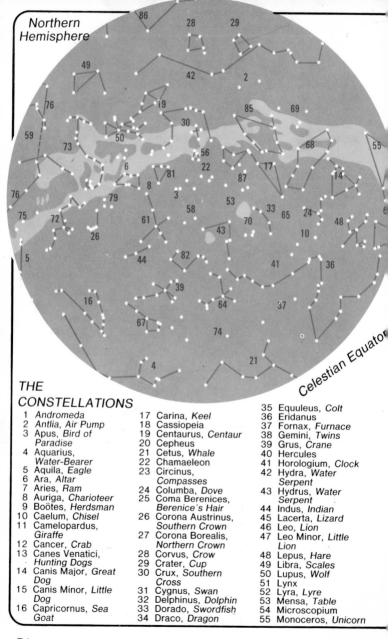

Northern Hemisphere

Celestian Equator

THE CONSTELLATIONS

1 Andromeda
2 Antlia, *Air Pump*
3 Apus, *Bird of Paradise*
4 Aquarius, *Water-Bearer*
5 Aquila, *Eagle*
6 Ara, *Altar*
7 Aries, *Ram*
8 Auriga, *Charioteer*
9 Boötes, *Herdsman*
10 Caelum, *Chisel*
11 Camelopardus, *Giraffe*
12 Cancer, *Crab*
13 Canes Venatici, *Hunting Dogs*
14 Canis Major, *Great Dog*
15 Canis Minor, *Little Dog*
16 Capricornus, *Sea Goat*

17 Carina, *Keel*
18 Cassiopeia
19 Centaurus, *Centaur*
20 Cepheus
21 Cetus, *Whale*
22 Chamaeleon
23 Circinus, *Compasses*
24 Columba, *Dove*
25 Coma Berenices, *Berenice's Hair*
26 Corona Austrinus, *Southern Crown*
27 Corona Borealis, *Northern Crown*
28 Corvus, *Crow*
29 Crater, *Cup*
30 Crux, *Southern Cross*
31 Cygnus, *Swan*
32 Delphinus, *Dolphin*
33 Dorado, *Swordfish*
34 Draco, *Dragon*

35 Equuleus, *Colt*
36 Eridanus
37 Fornax, *Furnace*
38 Gemini, *Twins*
39 Grus, *Crane*
40 Hercules
41 Horologium, *Clock*
42 Hydra, *Water Serpent*
43 Hydrus, *Water Serpent*
44 Indus, *Indian*
45 Lacerta, *Lizard*
46 Leo, *Lion*
47 Leo Minor, *Little Lion*
48 Lepus, *Hare*
49 Libra, *Scales*
50 Lupus, *Wolf*
51 Lynx
52 Lyra, *Lyre*
53 Mensa, *Table*
54 Microscopium
55 Monoceros, *Unicorn*

74

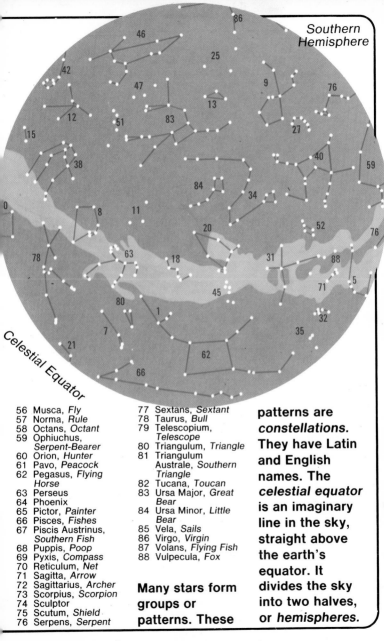

Southern Hemisphere

Celestial Equator

56 Musca, *Fly*
57 Norma, *Rule*
58 Octans, *Octant*
59 Ophiuchus, *Serpent-Bearer*
60 Orion, *Hunter*
61 Pavo, *Peacock*
62 Pegasus, *Flying Horse*
63 Perseus
64 Phoenix
65 Pictor, *Painter*
66 Pisces, *Fishes*
67 Piscis Austrinus, *Southern Fish*
68 Puppis, *Poop*
69 Pyxis, *Compass*
70 Reticulum, *Net*
71 Sagitta, *Arrow*
72 Sagittarius, *Archer*
73 Scorpius, *Scorpion*
74 Sculptor
75 Scutum, *Shield*
76 Serpens, *Serpent*

77 Sextans, *Sextant*
78 Taurus, *Bull*
79 Telescopium, *Telescope*
80 Triangulum, *Triangle*
81 Triangulum Australe, *Southern Triangle*
82 Tucana, *Toucan*
83 Ursa Major, *Great Bear*
84 Ursa Minor, *Little Bear*
85 Vela, *Sails*
86 Virgo, *Virgin*
87 Volans, *Flying Fish*
88 Vulpecula, *Fox*

Many stars form groups or patterns. These patterns are *constellations.* **They have Latin and English names. The** *celestial equator* **is an imaginary line in the sky,** straight above the earth's equator. It **divides the sky into two halves,** or *hemispheres.*

More Facts

Astronomy Firsts

About **4,000 B.C.** Chinese keep records of eclipses.

About **2,000 B.C.** Stonehenge (in England) is built for the study of astronomy.

About **A.D. 150** Ptolemy explains his theories about movements of the planets.

1543 Copernicus says that planets revolve around the sun.

1608 Hans Lippershey designs the first telescope.

1609 Galileo supports Copernicus' theory about the universe.

1668 Newton builds the first reflecting telescope.

1781 William Herschel discovers Uranus.

1877 Asaph Hall discovers the Martian moons Phobos and Deimos.

1918 100-inch (250 cm) Hooker telescope made at Mount Wilson observatory in California. Red shift discovered.

1930 Clyde Tombaugh discovers Pluto.

1931 Karl Jansky discovers radio waves from space.

1948 200-inch (500 cm) Hale telescope made at Palomar Observatory in California.

1957 Russia sends up *Sputniks 1* and *2*.

1958 U.S. sends up its first satellite, *Explorer 1*.

1960 Quasars are discovered.

1962 *Mariner 2* reports on Venus.

1965 *Mariner 4* takes first close-ups of Mars.

1967 Pulsars are discovered.

1969–'72 *Apollo* astronauts explore the moon.

1973 U.S. sends *Skylab* into space.

1976 *Viking* probes land on Mars.

1980 *Voyager 1* explores Jupiter and Saturn.

Sky Facts

Planet	Surface temperature	What the atmosphere is made of	Number of satellites
1. Mercury	779°F to 1,427°F (415°C to 775°C)	None	0
2. Venus	887°F (475°C)	Carbon dioxide	0
3. Earth	71.6°F (22°C)	Nitrogen, oxygen	1
4. Mars	−185°F to 86°F (−85°C to 30°C)	Carbon dioxide	2
5. Jupiter	−302°F (−150°C)	Hydrogen, helium	16
6. Saturn	−356°F (−180°C)	Hydrogen, helium	21
7. Uranus	−410°F (−210°C)	Hydrogen, helium, methane	5
8. Neptune	−428°F (−220°C)	Hydrogen, helium, methane	2
9. Pluto	−446°F? (−230°C)	Methane	0

Moon Facts

Diameter, equator:	2,155.2 miles (3,476 km)
Volume:	1/49 earth's volume
Average density:	3.34 (water = 1)
Mass:	1/81 earth's mass
Gravity:	1/6 earth's gravity
Average distance from earth:	238,080 miles (384,000 km)
Spins on axis in:	27⅓ days
Orbits earth in:	27⅓ days
New moon:	29½ days

THE LARGEST ASTEROIDS (rocks that orbit between Jupiter and Mars)

Ceres
621.8 miles across
(1,003 km)

Pallas
376.9 miles across
(608 km)

Vesta
333.6 miles across
(538 km)

Hygeia
229.4 miles across
(370 km)

Huge Telescopes

The bigger a telescope lens or mirror is, the more power the telescope has. And the bigger lens gives a clearer image. A telescope with a 4-inch (100 mm) diameter will bring together four times as much light as a telescope with a 2-inch (50 mm) diameter. The table on this page tells about some of the biggest telescopes.

It takes a long time and a lot of care to make mirrors or telescopes. The concave surface (a surface that curves in) must be within one-tenth of the wavelength of light.

Six Mirrors
The biggest mirrors are the hardest to make. So now, scientists are making a telescope with six mirrors instead of one. Each mirror is 1.98 yards (1.8 m) across. The six mirrors will do the work of one big one that measures 4.95 yards (4.5 meters).

This telescope will be at Mount Hopkins, Arizona. It will be the third most powerful telescope in the world. (See drawing at right.)

The Largest Optical Telescopes	Date Telescope Was Made
Aperture in yards	

(The aperture is the diameter of the lens or mirror of a telescope.)

6.6	Zelenchukskaya, Caucasus, USSR	1976
5.6	Mount Palomar, California	1948
4.4	Kitt Peak, Arizona	1973
4.4	Cerro Tololo, Chile	1976
4.29	Siding Spring, New South Wales, Australia	1975
4.18	Mauna Kea, Hawaii	1977
3.96	La Silla, Chile	1976
3.3	Mount Hamilton, California	1959
2.97	Fort Davis, Texas	1968
2.86	Crimea, USSR	1961
2.86	Byurakan, USSR	1973
2.75	Mount Wilson, California	1917

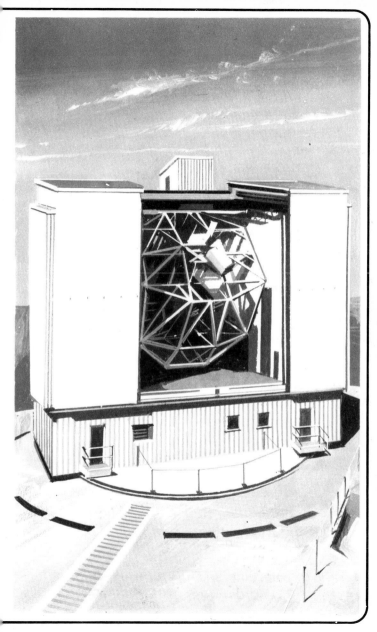

Flights Without People

Apollo moon landings and *Skylab* were piloted, or "manned," by astronauts. When there are no humans in the vehicles, they are "unmanned." Most studies in space have been done by unmanned vehicles.

The first probe to land on another planet was *Luna 2*. It reached the moon in 1959. Since then more than 30 probes have headed for other planets. *Viking 2* landed on Mars in 1976. In 1977 *Voyagers 1* and *2* spacecraft started on long trips to outer parts of the solar system. They passed Jupiter in 1979. In 1980 and 1981 they passed Saturn. *Voyager 2* is traveling on to Uranus and far-off Neptune. It will get to Neptune about 1989.

Space Telescope

A space shuttle flies back and forth between the earth and a space station. In 1983 the U.S. Space Shuttle will put a giant telescope in orbit.

The telescope in the space station will be able to tell us much more about the universe than telescopes on earth can. The Shuttle will be used to repair and service the telescope while it is in orbit.

The telescope will be able to see objects seven times farther away than those we can see from earth. These objects are so far away that light from them takes 14 billion years to get to us. Some scientists think the universe is that age!

Inside the Telescope

The space telescope will be 15.73 yards (14.2 m) long. Its diameter will be 5.17 yards (4.7 m).

Electric power will come from solar panels. (See drawing on right.)

Meteors and Comets

A meteor is a piece of stone or metal from space. Air makes the stone or metal hot. It glows. Even meteors the size of a pea can be bright. Most meteors are small. There are very, very few meteors big enough to hit the earth instead of burning up in the atmosphere.

On most nights you can see about five meteors every hour. Sometimes there are showers of meteors. They seem to spread out from a point in the sky. We call this point a **radiant.** The showers are named after the constellation in which the radiant lies.

The table on the next page tells you where and when to look for meteor showers.

Comets

Comets are much bigger than meteors. Most comets are a few miles across. Most are made of frozen gas and water mixed with dust.

The orbit of a comet is very long. A comet may travel from inside Mercury's orbit to outside Saturn's.

As the comet gets near the sun, it begins to melt. The comet's outer layers throw off clouds of material.

All of a sudden, a bright comet can come from nowhere. It blazes for a few months. Then, it goes out of sight. Maybe it will come back in a few thousand years.

Meteor Showers

Name of Shower	Where to Look	When to Look
Aquarids	Southwest of Pegasus	May 4-6
Geminids	Castor in Gemini	December 10-13
Leonids	Leo	November 16-18
Orionids	Between Orion and Gemini	October 18-22
Perseids	Perseus	August 10-12
Quadrantids	Between Boötes and Draco	January 1-3
Taurids	Between Taurus and Perseus	November 5-9

(Left) A meteor streaks through the sky.
(Above) The fiery path of a comet.

Comets

ENCKE's comet orbits between Jupiter and the sun. It comes back every 3.3 years.

HALLEY'S comet appears every 76 years. It will be here in 1986.

HUMASON comet was seen in 1961. We do not expect this big comet back before the year 4860.

IKEYA-SEKI comet was discovered in 1965.

Looking for Sunspots

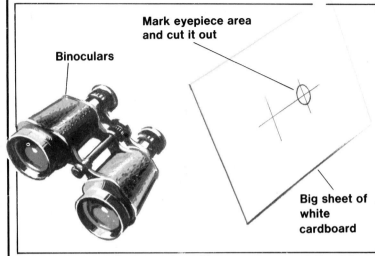

Binoculars

Mark eyepiece area and cut it out

Big sheet of white cardboard

Sunspots are dark spots that appear at certain times on the sun's surface. But we can't just look at the sun and try to find them. We must NEVER look straight up at the sun. We must NEVER look at it through binoculars or a telescope. If we do we may go blind.

There is a safe way to see sunspots. You need a pair of binoculars, two white cards, and some tape. Cut a hole in one of the cards. The hole should be big enough to fit around one of the binocular lenses. (You will use only one lens.)

Tape the binoculars firmly to the card. (See drawing.) Prop the binoculars on a chair by the window. Focus them on the other card until you have a clear image of the sun.

Do not focus the sun's image to a narrow point. That could set the card on fire!

You may see small black specks on the card. These are sunspots.

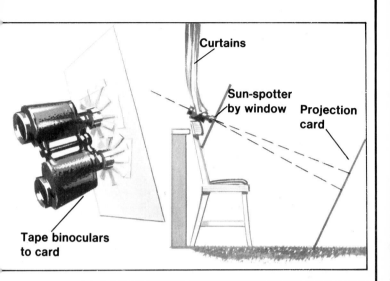

Curtains

Sun-spotter by window

Projection card

Tape binoculars to card

The image on the card may look like this. To make the image bigger, put the projection card farther from the spotter.

Sunspots are about 3,632° F (2,000° C) cooler than the rest of the sun's surface. That's why they are dark. They may cover several thousand square miles.

Photos of the Sky

Astronomers used to spend hours looking through telescopes. They studied one thing at a time. Now astronomers take photos through big telescopes. They take pictures of thousands of objects at once. Then they take all the time they want to study the photos.

Astronomers may need several hours to get an image on film. But if you want to take photos of the skies for a hobby, that's much easier.

Taking Photos

You will need a camera with a "Brief Time" (B) setting. When the camera is on this setting, the shutter stays open as long as the release button is pressed. Use the smallest aperture number. (The aperture is the hole that controls how much light gets to the film.) Focus on infinity. Make sure the camera is steady.

(Top) The camera was pointed at Polaris. The shutter was open a long time.

(Above) A man-made satellite crosses the stars.

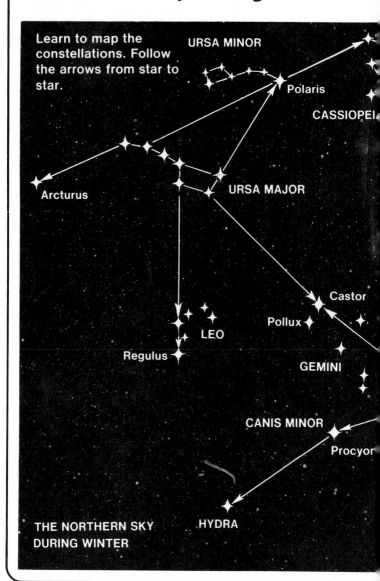

The North Sky at Night

Learn to map the constellations. Follow the arrows from star to star.

URSA MINOR

Polaris

CASSIOPEI

Arcturus

URSA MAJOR

Castor

Pollux

LEO

Regulus

GEMINI

CANIS MINOR

Procyor

HYDRA

THE NORTHERN SKY DURING WINTER

The earth spins on its axis. And it revolves around the sun. So the stars change their places from hour to hour and from month to month.

Capella

Pleiades

Aldebaran

Betel-
geuse

ORION

Rigel

Sirius

Many stars are in groups or patterns (**constellations**). Some constellations are easy to find. They help us find other stars and constellations.

The Big Dipper
The Big Dipper is another name for Ursa Major. It is a group of seven stars shaped like a deep pan with a curved handle. If we follow the curve of the handle, we find the bright star, Arcturus. Four stars make up the bowl of the dipper. Find the two stars that make the top and bottom of the side away from the handle. Imagine a line going through these two stars. The line starts at the bottom of the bowl. It goes past the top of the bowl. The North Star (Polaris) lies almost on this line.

From the Big Dipper, you can find the constellation Orion. It has two bright stars, Rigel and Betelgeuse. The three stars of Orion's belt point south to Sirius. Sirius is the brightest star.

Finding the Planets

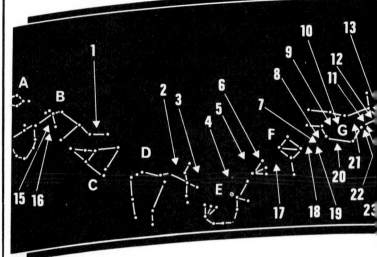

Long ago people watched objects moving around in the sky. They called them planets. "Planet" is a Greek word for something that wanders. Planets weren't like stars, which seemed to stay in the same place.

People thought that stars were set on the inside of a great black globe. They thought the earth was inside this globe. The people saw that planets passed through certain constellations in a narrow band of sky. This band of sky is the **zodiac.** There are twelve constellations in the zodiac. Planets stay in the zodiac as they go around the sun in oval-shaped orbits.

The Bright Ones

The four brightest planets are Venus, Jupiter, Mars, and Saturn. The diagram above will help you find them. After you find a constellation of the zodiac, any extra "star" you see will be a planet.

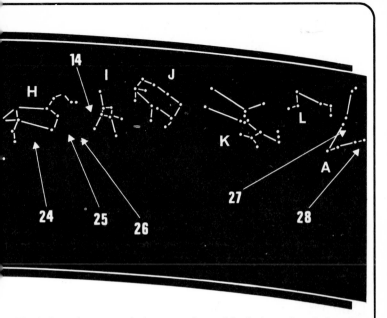

Find the planet and date on the table below. Look for the number listed in the table in the drawing above. The letters in the drawing go with the constellations in the list at the bottom of this page.

		Venus	Mars	Jupiter	Saturn
1981	Fall	19	14	23	13
1982	Spring	1	12	8	11
	Fall	22	17	7	21
1983	Spring	27	28	5	9
	Fall	26	25	6	10
1984	Spring	15	16	2	18
	Fall	24	4	3	20

A Pisces   E Scorpius   I Cancer
B Aquarius   F Libra   J Gemini
C Capricornus   G Virgo   K Taurus
D Sagittarius   H Leo   L Aries

Index